Hot and Cold

Contents

Hot and cold	2
Poem	3
The effects of heat	4
Expansion	6
Freezing	8
Ice	10
Thermometers	12
What is heat?	14
The work of Count Rumford and Humphry Davy	
Heat travels	18
Working with heat	20
Heat and life	22
Glossary	24

Hot and cold

What do you mean when you say something is hot or cold? We can mean different things at different times. Something that seems warm to one person, is cold to another.

Imagine . . .
You are in a swimming pool. The water feels just right – not cold at all. But if the same water was in your bath, you wouldn't like it; it would feel too cold.

If you swim in the main swimming pool, it feels warm enough. But, if you then go into the toddlers' pool it feels very warm. When you return to the large pool, it feels very cold. Why do you think that is?

Imagine...
You have been outside on a cold winter's day. You come indoors. The house feels warm and cosy. But everyone else is complaining that it is cold. It is warmer than it was outside, so to you the house feels warm.

Because it is so hard to guess how hot or cold something is, we need a way to measure heat and cold. Otherwise we can only say 'hotter than' or 'colder than'. Is your kitchen warmer than your bedroom? Is the fridge colder than the garden?

Chips

Out of the paper bag
Comes the breath of the chips
And I shall blow on them
To stop them burning my lips.

Before I leave the counter
The woman shakes
Raindrops of vinegar on them
And salty snowflakes.

Outside the frosty pavements
Are slippery as a slide
But the chips and I
Are warm inside.

Stanley Cook

The effects of heat

Heat changes things. These changes may last for ever, or they might be changes that can be reversed. Then things return to the way they were.

If you make a piece of wood hot enough, it will burn. When you burn a piece of wood, it turns to smoke, gases and ashes. It can never be changed back into wood.

When you make a cake, the raw mixture is wet and sticky. But when it is heated and cooked, it becomes spongy and dry. It cannot be turned back into cake mixture. You cannot 'uncook' it and make it raw again.

Many other things are changed by cooking. Raw eggs are soft and runny, but cooked ones are hard and rubbery. Raw vegetables are hard and crisp, but cooked ones are softer.

Once these foods have been heated and cooked, they cannot go back to how they were when they were raw. Can you think of any other things that change for ever when they are heated?

Some things melt when they are heated. Wax, fat, chocolate, butter and ice all melt when they are made hot enough. They change from being solid to liquid. But when they cool down, they become solid again.

What other things can you think of that melt in heat? When they cool down, do they go back to how they were before?

Water seems to vanish when it is heated. It turns to gas called **steam**. When this happens, we say the water has **evaporated**. Steam turns back to water when it is cooled down. The cloud from the spout of a boiling kettle that we call 'steam', is really a cloud of tiny drops of water caused by the steam cooling.

Watch a kettle when it is boiling. Can you see the white cloud of tiny water drops? Where is it? The white cloud does not start immediately at the end of the spout. There is steam in the place where you can see nothing. The cloud starts at the place where the steam starts to cool to water drops.

Water drops

Steam

Expansion

Heat makes things get bigger or expand. These people are building a motorway bridge.

"Look. We're leaving small gaps between each section of the bridge. We do this because the bridge will get longer in hot weather."

"If there were no gaps, it would buckle and bend and that would be the end of the bridge. But, with these gaps, the bridge can expand safely."

Can you think of a way of using hot water to help you open a tight bottle cap? What happens to the metal?

Railway tracks are also laid with gaps between them. That's because in hot weather the metal expands. The gaps allow room for the tracks to expand safely without bumping into each other. If there were no gaps, the tracks would bend and buckle in hot weather and cause dangerous accidents.

Nowadays, railway tracks are often laid in much longer lengths without many gaps. The problem of expansion during hot weather is avoided because the tracks are fixed to heavy concrete sleepers which stop the tracks moving.

Have you ever heard furniture creaking at night? During the day, the furniture gets warm and expands slightly but at night, it cools down and shrinks. As it shrinks, it creaks!

When you fry sausages or bake potatoes in their jackets, you have to prick holes in their skins. Why do you think you have to do this?

Waverley Station, Edinburgh

Freezing

When water becomes very cold, it freezes and becomes solid. When water has got cold enough to freeze, we say it has reached its 'freezing-point'.

When unfrozen food is left in a warm place for too long, it is attacked by tiny living things called **bacteria**. These make food go bad. Bad food tastes and smells horrible and can make you very ill. When fresh food is frozen, the bacteria stop working and the food stays fresh. Before you eat frozen food, you have to thaw it and cook it, if it needs cooking.

We can keep food fresh for a longer period of time by freezing it. The water in the food freezes, making the food hard and very cold. When it is frozen, the food can be kept for a long time without going bad. What frozen foods do you prepare and eat at home?

How long do different liquids take to freeze? Try testing some different liquids such as water, salty water and milk. How can you make your test fair?

Milk freezes too when it gets cold enough. If you have milk delivered in bottles to your doorstep, you might see it frozen on very cold days. Milk expands when it freezes. That's why the top of the frozen milk sticks out of the bottle.

Gases, as well as liquids, will freeze when they get to the right temperature. A gas called carbon dioxide is sometimes frozen. It becomes solid 'dry ice'. It is much colder than ordinary ice. It is so cold that if you touch it, it can feel as if it is burning you.

When dry ice is warmed up, it does not melt. It turns back into gas. When it turns back into gas, it looks white and smoky. People often use dry ice in the theatre or at pop concerts to look like smoke.

Ice

Imagine you have travelled back in time a million years. You land in Siberia in the north of Russia. You look out of your time-machine and see a huge, hairy animal rather like an elephant. In fact, it is a mammoth, making its way across the snow.

Suddenly, it slips and falls into a crack in the ice. It dies and would rot away, but the ice freezes its body.

A million years later, the frozen body of the mammoth is found in Siberia. It still has the food that it had eaten in its stomach. Because the body had frozen, it has not decayed or rotted away. It looks as if it died only a few weeks ago!

Model of a woolly mammoth

Icebergs can be enormous! Even so, you can only see the part of an iceberg that's above water—there's more than three-quarters of it hidden underwater.

Icebergs in the Arctic vary in size, from the size of a large piano to the size of a ten-storey building. An iceberg the size of a piano is called a 'growler' and icebergs the size of small houses are called 'bergy bits'.

Make an ice balloon! Fill a balloon with water and tie the end firmly. Put it in a carrier bag (in case it bursts) and put it in the freezer. It will take two or three days to freeze. Tear off the balloon when the water is frozen.

There are lots of things you can do with your balloon: look at it, float it, put it in warm water, paint it, put salt on it. What else can you think of? When you float your balloon, how much of it is below water and how much is above water?

The Inuit people live in the far north of America. They build homes from blocks of earth. A few years ago, a hut was found buried in ice. It had the frozen bodies of a family in it. The hut and the bodies had been there for over 100 years, preserved perfectly by the cold.

Present-day Inuit people in their home

Thermometers

We have difficulty in telling how hot or cold things are, so we use thermometers. We use them to measure **temperature**. There are a number of different kinds of thermometer. They each have different uses.

Alcohol thermometers are used to measure how hot or cold the air is. They are long, glass tubes which contain a liquid called alcohol. Red colouring is added to the alcohol. As the air gets warmer, the liquid expands and rises up the narrow tube. The hotter it is, the higher the liquid rises. We read the temperature from the top of the liquid.

Alcohol thermometers are only useful for measuring room temperatures. We use thermometers filled with a liquid metal called mercury for measuring higher temperatures. The mercury rises in the tube as it gets hotter, just as the alcohol does.

We measure temperature in **degrees**. We call the freezing point of water zero degrees Celsius. Boiling water is usually 100 degrees Celsius. We write it like this: 100°C. This way of measuring heat and cold is used in almost every country in the world.

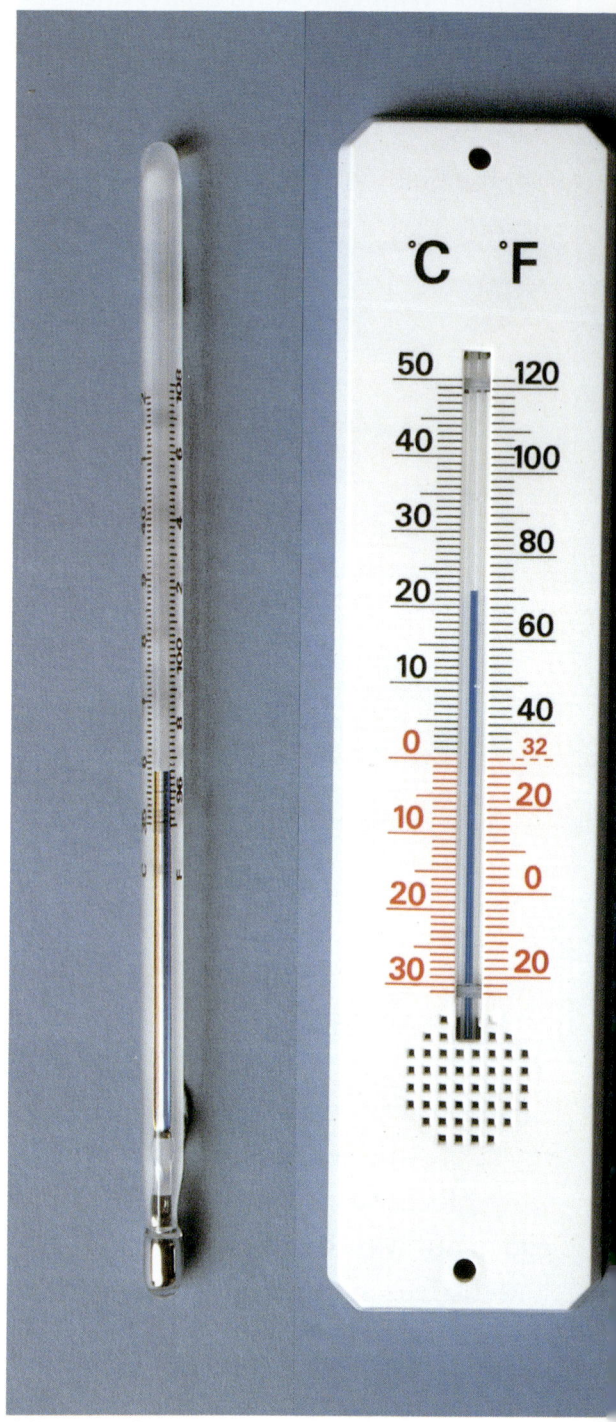

Mercury thermometer   Alcohol thermometer

Clinical thermometers are used for measuring the temperature of the human body. There is a tiny bend in the tube to prevent the mercury from falling back after the thermometer is removed from the mouth. After you have read the temperature, you have to shake the thermometer to make the mercury go back. Your body temperature should be about 37°C. If it is higher than that, you are probably ill.

Nowadays, we often use liquid crystal thermometers. They change colour with the change of temperature. You press one to your forehead and the colour changes to tell you your temperature. Some drivers use liquid crystal thermometers as an ice alert. They have one stuck to the wing mirror of their car. When the temperature outside gets so cold that the roads might be icy, they can see the colour change.

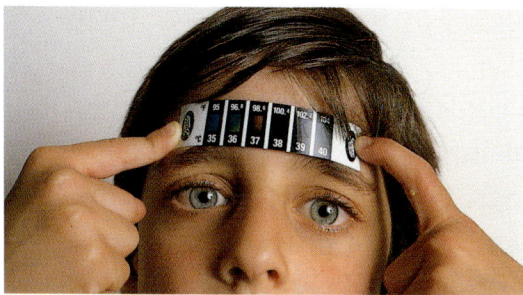

Liquid crystal thermometer

Place an ordinary mercury thermometer in very cold water. Read the temperature at the top of the mercury while the thermometer is still in the water. Now remove the thermometer from the water. Keep looking at the mercury level. What happens? Why do you think this is happening? Why is it important to keep the thermometer in the water when you are taking the temperature of the water?

Do the same thing again, but this time use hot water from the tap.

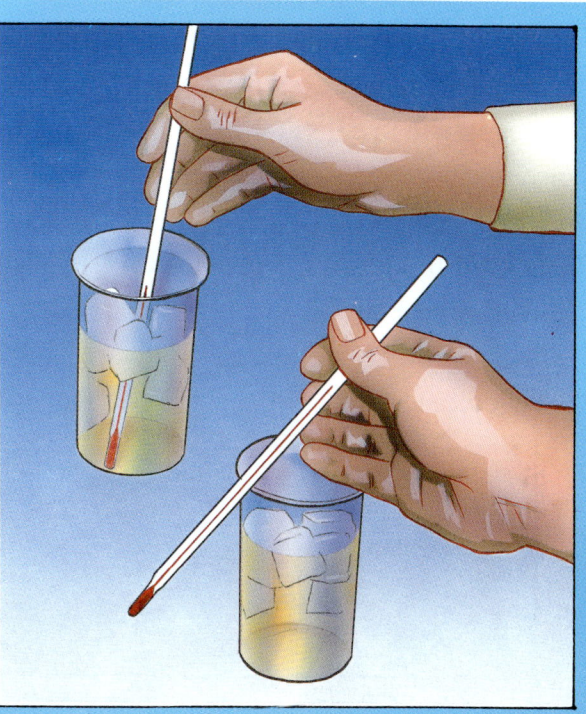

What is heat?

Everyone knows what 'hot' means. Everyone knows what 'cold' means. But what is 'heat'?

For hundreds of years, people thought that heat was a liquid. It was invisible, but it was there. Hot things held more of it than cold things. The heat-liquid made them hot.

People used the idea of invisible heat-liquid to explain all kinds of things. For example, they said that when you put a kettle of water on the flames of a fire, heat-liquid flowed from the flames into the water. It made the water hot. If you were silly enough to stick your finger in the fire, heat-liquid flowed into you instead of the water. It burned you. When you took the kettle off the flames, heat-liquid flowed out of the water into the air. The air grew warmer, and the water grew colder.

For hundreds of years, people accepted the idea of heat-liquid. No one asked questions about it. No one asked, "Why can't we see heat-liquid? Why should we believe that it's there at all? We need proof!"

Then, about two hundred years ago, two scientists carried out some experiments. They wanted to see what heat was really like. The first scientist, Count Rumford, worked in a gun factory. The factory made cannons. First, metal for the cannons was poured into moulds. It set into a cannon-shape with a wide hole down the middle for the cannon-balls. When the metal was cool, workers drilled small holes at one end, ready to hold gunpowder.

Count Rumford noticed that as the workmen drilled the holes, the cannon-metal grew hotter. This could not be because heat-liquid was flowing from the drill into the cannon-metal. The drill was cold to begin with. It had no heat-liquid in it. Yet, when the drilling was finished, both the drill and the cannon-metal were hotter. It was the movement of the drill that made them hotter. There was no heat-liquid at all. This puzzled him—he wondered if heat was movement.

The second heat-scientist was Humphry Davy. He read about Count Rumford's idea that heat was movement, not liquid, and thought about it.

He did an experiment to prove it. He took two lumps of ice. He held each of them with tongs. Then he rubbed them together. As he rubbed, the ice began to melt. It was impossible for heat-liquid to be flowing from one piece of ice to the other. The ice was cold: it had no heat-liquid in it.

Both pieces of ice are cold but they are melting. It must be the movement which is melting the ice. So heat must be something to do with movement.

Modern scientists still agree with Count Rumford and Humphry Davy. They believe that heat is a kind of movement. The idea works. The old idea worked until someone proved it wrong. Our ideas can change all the time. 'Keep thinking'—that's what we have to do.

Heat travels

Heat travels in different ways.

The heat from the flames in this bonfire makes the smoke and ash drift upwards. When the ash has cooled down, it falls to the ground.

Hot air rises through cold air. The hot air that is trapped in this balloon makes it float upwards through the cooler air.

Heat travels through some solid things more quickly than others. On a hot day, would you rather sit on a metal chair or a canvas chair? And on which chair would you rather sit on a cold day? Metal can take heat away from the body but other materials, like paper, help heat stay in the body.

Can you think of a way to test different materials to see which ones heat spreads through more quickly?

Insulation

Heat travels through solid things as well as through the air. The heat spreads from the hot parts of something to the cooler parts. So, the part of a metal teaspoon that is sticking out of a hot drink, will feel hot. The heat from the tea makes the part of the spoon that is in the drink hot. The heat then spreads up the handle of the spoon.

Materials that allow heat to spread quickly are **good conductors**. Materials that do not allow heat to spread quickly are **poor conductors**.

Wood is a poor conductor. Heat travels through it slowly. Saucepan handles are often made of wood. They stay cool while the pan is too hot to touch. Can you think of any other good or poor conductors?

We can use poor conductors as **insulation**. When something is warm, insulation will help to keep it warm. But when something is cold, insulation will help to keep it cold.

Can you test a variety of materials to find out whether or not they are good insulators?

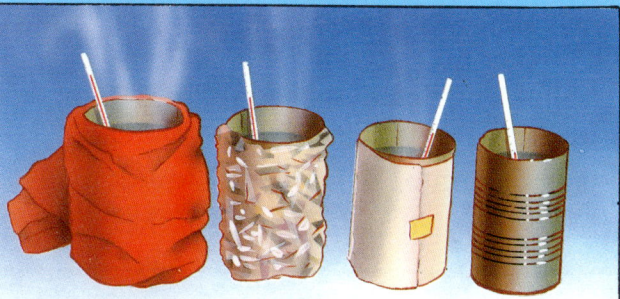

Working with heat

Metal smelting

Glass-making

Heat is very useful to us. We use it for cooking, for getting warm and for drying things. Heat is also used in industry to help make things.

Heat can be used to get metals from the rocks or **ores** where they are found. For example, iron is found in iron ore. The ore is heated in a furnace. Hot air, up to 1600°C, is blasted into the furnace. Liquid iron is formed and runs out of the furnace. This process is called **smelting**.

Glass is made from a sandy substance called silica. Like metal, silica melts when it is heated. Unlike metal, it can become clear or see-through. **Molten** (melted) glass is poured around moulds to make bottles.

You can heat plastic so that it melts. The melted plastic can then

"I'm a blacksmith. I make steel shoes for horses. These stop their hooves from wearing out on hard road surfaces."

"I heat a steel bar until it is red hot. Steel bends more easily when it is red hot."

"I bend and hammer each shoe until it fits the horse perfectly."

"I fit the shoe to the horse when it is hot. It doesn't hurt the horse and it fits the hoof perfectly."

be poured into moulds to make objects of almost any shape and size.

Clay also changes when it is heated. Plates, dishes, cups, saucers and bricks are all made of soft, damp clay. It is dried out and then baked in a very, very hot oven, called a kiln. As the clay is baked, it changes colour and becomes much harder. It has been changed for ever. It can never become soft clay again.

These bathroom fittings are made of clay.

Heat and life

The bodies of some animals are the same temperature as the air or water around them. So, if it is cold, the insides and outsides of their bodies are cold. To become active, these animals need to be warmed by the sun. Although their blood is not always cold, we call these animals **cold-blooded**.

Sometimes you can see cold-blooded animals like butterflies or lizards, lying in sunny places getting warm.

Other animals, like birds and mammals, keep their bodies the same temperature, however cold or hot it is outside. We say that these animals are **warm-blooded**. Humans are warm-blooded animals. That means that your body temperature is always more or less the same, unless you are ill.

Warm-blooded animals have to keep their bodies warm in cold weather. Birds have feathers which insulate them against the cold. Mammals usually have hair or fur to keep them warm. Whales have a thick layer of fat called blubber. This keeps them warm, even in really cold water.

Iguana

African elephant

Mammals must keep cool in hot weather. People do this by sweating. The damp sweat helps keep us cool in hot weather or when we take exercise. Dogs lose most of their heat by panting with their mouths open. They cool down when the water, or saliva, on their tongues evaporates. Elephants do the same sort of thing by flapping their ears.

Birds' eggs must be kept warm or they will not hatch. Usually, the parent birds keep the eggs warm by sitting on them. But some birds have other methods! If you've ever dug inside a compost heap or felt inside a pile of grass cuttings, you'll know it's very warm inside. The incubator bird from Australia makes a mound of earth and dead leaves, up to five metres high. The rotting leaves make the mound hot. The bird lays its eggs in the mound and leaves them to incubate.

Swans

Some other animals lay eggs too. Snakes lay eggs and some snakes bury their eggs in leaves to keep them warm.

Loggerhead turtles lay their eggs in the sand on a beach The temperature of the sand affects the way the eggs hatch. If it goes above 30°C, most eggs will hatch out as females. If it goes below 28°C, most are males.

Glossary

bacteria
Bacteria are some of the tiny living things that are too small to see without a microscope. There are both useful and harmful bacteria.

cold-blooded
The body and blood temperature of cold-blooded animals changes according to the temperature of the outside environment. These animals do not necessarily have cold blood.

degree
The unit of measurement of temperature.

to evaporate
When a liquid changes to a gas, it evaporates.

good conductor
A substance which heat or electricity or other forms of energy pass through easily.

insulation
The way in which we limit the passage of heat or electricity or other forms of energy in or out of something.

molten
A solid is molten when it becomes so hot that it melts and becomes liquid.

ore
An ore is a rock which contains metal.

poor conductor
A substance which heat or electricity or other forms of energy do not pass through easily.

smelting
The process of taking metal out of ores using heat.

steam
When water evaporates, it turns into a gas called steam. Steam is invisible.

temperature
The measurement of the hotness or coldness of something.

warm-blooded
The body and blood temperature of warm-blooded animals stays more or less the same whatever the temperature of the outside environment.